NINETY-SIX TEARS

Michael Gottlieb

ROOF

NINETY-SIX TEARS is published as ROOF XIII, vol. 4, no. 1, partly through a grant from the Coordinating Council of Literary Magazines as well as donations from individuals and sales of other publications.

Cover: *1200 Broadway, 1974* by Richard Haas. Courtesy of the artist and Brooke Alexander, Inc., New York. Special thanks to Michael Heming.

ISBN 0-937804-07-x

ROOF BOOKS
are published by
The Segue Foundation
300 Bowery
New York, N.Y. 10012

To My Parents

Ninety-Six Tears

I.

The little death, first. There is no such thing as an emergency in the poetry world. Trained on. Like a third armpit. The advantage of the cordless model. You went and had all this shipped in. Promoting camaraderie. And didn't think to ask me if I needed any notions. Duty

Tour in a 'hot.' Deep enough so no one would notice. In fact, not foundationless red herrings. Play in traffic. I have dollars tonight. But closer approximations of what only a few knew in actuality. Scram. Shove off. Go fan it. Major repairs. Get lost. Make like Houdini. A show

Cause order. In line. Somewhere in the Dominican Republic. Steak fries. The American plan. Purloined and subsequently repainted and furnished with new serial numbers, for the fourth time. An admit list in addition to a guest list. The almost vaudevillian realization that all those

Rightist paranoid fantasies. Beat it. Go take the air. All serving as witting dupes. Convection summary. The fickle incandescent. Devouring the characterization. Bought or sold, were. Take a walk. The techs and the temps. All walks of life. Basque cocktail lounge. The shame of God.

Professional banquettes. There was nothing really left downtown. In all fairness. Betsy hates les Bourbons. Do you think I have eyes in the back of my head. I mean, I ran over to that cab. Make friends with yourself. The subjects who cannot be left alone. It was clear that most had.

Witness the dapper oarman. Cancel service anytime. On the outside. For love or money. Ballast from the Catskills. Perhaps a few weeks. Renting the moon. Eases smoker's throat. If that, by his lights. One could tell by the telephone doodles. Swatting revisionists. Jovian anxie-

Ty. She, as if she hadn't a. Belonging to an ex-boxer. This will explain everything. This abject cast. Listening to you. Crip pics. All season. An orphaned gesture. Is like having all my problems aired in terms of Greek theatre. A way with words you'd like to remember. Someone who wore t

Shirts underneath, even in August. Crafty little bittern. Cashiered. Your cenotaph. A smile and a shoeshine. Treatise on lifting and separating, effortlessly. I appreciate your disdain. No gushy spills. Get a line on it. I just wanted to show you. The Framers. An epistomological

Downturn. One of those with baby skin and steel hair. Beats me. Four walling. Abrogating the struggle for form in favor of an Advent and a Laserdisc. "Would you mind vacating the premises?" As cool as. A dent in their. Moose. Hopes. Dialysis banter. In the saddle. Cowering behind

The salt cellar. Abnegation as a tactic. Genial anguish. Chocked up. So that, if we know that they. A change of clothes. That whole segment of the world. The flimsiest caprice of hope of there being a locus of *sanity* we could, if not quite attach ourselves to. Our last platform for any sup-

Position. And then. Also. In accepting this. Safe house. Like a dauber. As out to lunch, as it were, as any of them. As it seems necessitous. In a way that only becomes clearer. As we get to know eachother or like or need eachother more. Individually and as a group. Coming to the

Realization. That we. And we are. More for all the ridiculousness that year by year. The dawn of creation. And ourselves and eachother. You didn't pay me to be caustic. Like an air of debacle. A sofa like the one he dimly recollected from another childhood. We, too, are or must appear

Objective. Craning the antennae. We are convinced that this *they* is a juggernaut totally out of control. A lineal escarpment. Some sense of compulsion to return all those calls. Close to a tryst. Then, as it were, aim ourselves. That we have developed such an elegant critique of all.

The luggage of everything he once held so. Deep dish. Pantechnicon misanthropy. Duct tape. Trust your gut feelings. For, in such a way so as to give us pause. Spooning in the middle of the tunnel. Any advantage. Like remembering how to ride a bicycle. Or any advantageous position.

Reshuffled prexies. A worn jantzen next to a pool in Great Neck. Of access or observation for gathering, as it were. All that which we can delineate and demean as *they*. As it were, evidence, for the production of an indictment. Feets got to dance. On anyone else. Put that in your

Pipedream. Presenting a statement regarding how soi-disant. Perfidious servitors. They felt. Haggling over her fate. Another kind of loanout. I think I may have something coming up for you. Breaking his vow. "I'm too drunk to talk to you." Snorting rice crispies. They are getting bored

With eachother. She's a public service. Unfair. Announcement. Yenning. Blurbiste. Panged. And. Fecks. Dammitall. Monic design. One of the best. Lap. Flechette. Knackery. Weekend evening. Heaping. For this sort. Monday through. Blamed. Galling. Fine. Unseating. Gainsay.

Skein. Rant. Coruscating. Dirty blonde. Stoll dollar. Ranking fob.Yeggs. Unalloyed. Sheer off. Ignudi. Nailer. Aforesworn. Limbic. Gloomy. Informers' corner. Ramps. Lettish regiments. Half life of the school. Had. Cavilling. Deny. Underwriters Laboratories. Bearer. Gaol.

Carryover. Indicative. Follow up. Unlain. Corneal. Better. Professed. Even better than your signature. Rotary fire. Your likeness on a treasury note. Tan. Waits in the heavens. Let's put it in the coal chute. I've been wanting to tell you how much I loved your party favors, who would have

Thought. Used to be an active. Matchsticks could be put in so many interesting places. Member. Any old color. Deferred all his points. Industrial wire shelving. But I've been so busy. Compare these estimates. 1,000 Worldwide Stamps. Are you kidding, this is great for my career.

Overtly paired. It's mine. A new door. Witting accomplice. The drop dead look. Unpinned. Tonier in the bush. Showpiece. Wasn't sure if it was really an argument. The paths near the gondola terminus. The show that X's cousin has so, as it were, passionately curated. Meadow of

Slacks. Stone deaf. The central minds. Janisseries dozing. Painting the flashing. Because of the retort. What happened last night, I'm trying not to think, again such (did or didn't) and so, went up on, don't motion, half once, eyeing, a bench in the yard, ranks on. Incidental abuse

Curve. Racking her brain. Winging the drummer. A stretch Subaru. That an indiscreet comeback could wreak such havoc. May my map cleave to the roof. The golden load. Free Tonga Banana Stamp And 100 Other Genuine Rare Postage Stamps. Capricious routines. Isn't my idea

Of a boffo time. Ask Andy Hardy. While someone else is spilling their brew on my new shoes. The subsuming of the overweening in prescriptive toil. Having someone scream *Cindy* in my ear for half an hour. Coming back to the world. "I don't know anything about you." That

Feeling in the morning, sometimes a peculiar filtre, vague haze, a nonassignable, of dread. Commercial invective. In Ethiopia or the Sudan. Exercises in taking us out to lunch. The last of the incontinent. Basically a packager. The drop on the rope. Reclining on the hood of a

Buick in front of Duane-Reade. Those so-called dirtbags. Spare haircut. A rendezvous with ineptness. All markets except Yugoslavia and South-West Africa. Hence the smudge and the bruises. It tried to whirl away and slipped. Trying to floor them with debatedly attuned cold snaps of

Caustically observational. Gelginite for the Holidays. Erstwhile frenzy. Crake. Best boy. A bit a' alright. Sluggard. Storm drain. Corten toiletries. Dispirited Fredericus. Grifters. Reorder fiber. Minnowing. I think you can take it. Perspex. Timely contortions. Normalization in-

Come. Driving to distraction, speeding tickets included. The way his eyelid refused to. Intrepid mollusk. Trompe d'oeil grain elevators. I mean something like this, the Last Range, incredible locations. We get hold of one of the reuseable ones, an entire astrological angle to exploit.

Like in Moonraker. Something on the order of the Hallmark Hall of Fame or the Bell Telephone Hour. We'll make our nut back before the first day, or orbit, of production. With a service industry/country and western angle. Terrific flack. We fit them out in shiny suits and mini

Cams, one of those dance companies, we'll punch our own ticket. A whiff of springtime. "Cocktails continuously." Swapping tweezer jokes. Calumnity anatomy. Puffy centuries. He was there hopefully. Sophomore votaries. No wires. Complete mobility. It is buyable. The

Drab deportment. I don't think you should see him anymore. An appeals screening. At the headwaters. For lack of anything better to do. Acerbic strapping. Inconsiderate sniper. As well as other adventurisms, leading many to wonder at the general acuity of whatever operation

Mayhap otherwise be engaged in, revealing a fidelity, which upon the rare occasion of their airing, what you don't realize, are loudspeakers, behind all those unobtrusive grills. Fourteen beers. Your loft and the phone booth I just happened to be passing by. Satan's luncheonette.

Bill me for the intervening issues. This could be your big break. An opera of unallocatable affections. Detect Truth and Deception. Protect your Privacy. Disguise your voice against eavesdroppers. Watch out for that safe. A green pig in a green poke. As he listened he realized he was

Hearing someone else read the poem he had been waiting all his life to write. Addled naps. Battalions of volunteers. A predictable procedural. A used fruit jar. Not really expecting you'd be home anymore, I just kept going to the phone when I came to the end of a chapter. Electronic

Mind Reader. Can be assessed for Truth or Lies. A matter of form. Then I kept calling to 2:00 am. Just to stretch my back. Development and printing. Throat to rage. When you finally get what you want now, what you'll be wanting then. No Attachments to Subjects necessary.

Correctable testimonials. The seventh generator. No, it's borrowed. Something to make up for the general lack of perfection. A bill in hand. Fidgety delegations. "I'm sure glad I didn't have to pay to listen to this." More like a Derange A Trois. The roadies' improprieties. "You

Owe me." Basement reasoning. Like a cyst. Ability to organize and present ideas in a clear and effective written form. Ability to handle a complex flow of work involving frequent interaction with other staff. The flattened edge of the top of the sack fitted under the door to his room,

The lucky one getting ready to jump up and down. After chip and bubble comes vapor. First filling a brown paper bag with medicated shaving cream. Until it became obvious that he was holding back the act. Contractural dubiety. Trounced by the crafts. In the wall of the rock face he

Really thought he was erecting in front of his work. Depressing reductor elision. As if there was no distinction in one's writing habits. Unalterable markings. Another callous glad handing provincial Gauleiter. His uncritical baggage. Some later swarms of grubbers would

Find it just as obligatory to find epiphanal moods in what one intended to appear as totally noncommital. As much as or more than any similar body of work for its time. Going into massive debt for a new loved one. Assimilated and eventually acclimatized to the inevitability.

"Retailing" intake. Half of what the government wants. Cafes as safe as freeways. I didn't want to have to ask that person to sit there for so long, but, on the other hand. Graeco roman pests. Dancey asylums. That you weren't sufficiently in control of your schedule to keep yourself from

Getting caught up in those sort of tiresome social chores, it isn't easy to tell you this but your initial error was in exhibiting just that vulnerability to her blandishments. A sort of noise, 4:30 in the morning, I can tell by the way your phone rings, and, in a way a susceptability to those wiles.

Doesn't finally end up bothering me as it used to, the way between the rings themselves there is that empty sound of creaking, making tracks, silently warning you of a Transmitter hidden in your presence. I can sort of block it out, which you would rather see as a manifestation of your

Disarming candor, for example. And the snap of ginger ale bottles opening. In a way you had her going until you reluctantly told her that not only could you not get out of that appointment conflict and spend time with her instead. And manage, on my poor camp cot, even in a

God forsaken night like this. That tells me not only are you not alone on this line. But, eventually, to find some comfort. But you had to go further, and, in assuring her how much you would rather pass the time with her, don't you see how much, on your own, without any

Unreasonable prompting, you gave up to her? Like a mass analysis of the way to hail a cab. If she didn't exactly expect you to lord it over her for being so solidly booked. Send this one to the cleaners. Then she surely didn't want to hear, no matter how superficially flatteringly you meant

It. During the eighteenth Brumaire. Perhaps this is the time to check out. What you are going through doesn't surprise me in the least. Or say how easily you are willing to be satisfied. Taciturn sewers. When it goes into turnaround. Demission. It troubles me when you admit how sim-

Ply. Thanks for the book and here's what I've been up to lately. Patmo-sian formulae. The hook of the. Melancholic ashtray. Consumptive pasterns. A different sort of infraction, verging, employments in the dative accusative. Bases in East Texas that only a few folks in Maryland

Have ever heard about. Choleric. Fractious. Rancorous. If someone makes me the right offer, sure I will. Pale green in the stains that fell below the bronze or brass bases which once supported poles for stan-dards. Phone Guard tells you it's safe to talk. Kinds of ambivalance

Found in upper middle class jewish third generation ne'erdowells. Using Dr. Scholl's adhesive corn plasters on either side of the bridge of the nose. "Writing less makes me more conscious of my calling as a poet." Phone Privacy, do you have it, are you sure? Shake well, touch on, do

Not brush. It'll make more money if it never breaks even. The satisfaction of knowing someone's shaved twice in one day for you. Bar clocks, over 2½ ft. high and twenty minutes fast. Why are you doing this to me? I need someone to get me out of this chair. Maroon ideation. A way

Of showing one's lineage and class loyalty. No so much as always out to lunch, it was more like she was on permanent separate vacations. Hectic adumbration. Something one needs to do at least three times a week, at our age. Take your thumb and sit on it. Bugged?, Revolutionary New

Privacy Device. Comprehensive Report and Surveillance and Counter Measures. This way of showing your feelings. An entailed narrative. As apart from doing it, actually, yourself. Getting it back, the patience of the fearing. A pin holding in place the wig of personality. Sure I can

Write a sentence as long as anyone here. I wanted to put you in the position of wanting me more. The blue swell. Collecting never to be used orange juice tops and seals, or, likewise, trying to clean up the beer stains before leaving for the movies with guests. An inducement like a

Recruiter's. Tastes left in the mouth. Our shared interest rate. Not completely in control of one's breath, longer or shorter. The way it always going along the ribbon of the plan. Proceeding from the given that this was what I cared to want. Heartily sick of this p.a. shuck. This is indeed

The kind of life you have been pointing yourself toward, you should have realized years ago, after all I have done to try and make you see. Chances for good photo opportunities. Persuaded with a little old fashioned. A certain type at the doors. Those who write as opposed to

Those who think. Familiarity with germane substantive and organizational issues. Fading into the small appliance section. The budding canopy. Not excoriating the sky. Bankrolling. Ability to work independently and carry out tasks and projects without detailed instruc-

Tion and supervision. Something we should both decide to need. Since the analysis we had developed, accounting for the neglect we had found ourselves in, which dissected what we saw as the generalized modes of the production of meaning, subsuming within itself neatly, while it was

At it, just about everyone except ourselves, in which, it seemed, issues of control and acceptable behavior were implemented into the syntax of the very atmosphere, into every declension of reality, as also, a precise and neat explanation of, simultaneously, the abject *boringness* and op-

Pression of all the surroundings and our distance from any meaningful centers or foci from which to effect any possible change, or merely make ourselves heard, kinds of change, obviously precluded because of the manifest danger we posed, by our example, and our work. Interestingly,

It turns out that since this analysis dovetailed so cleanly into our situation the only way to enjoy reinforcement (of it) was to continuously butt our heads, after a fashion, against those same unreceptive walls; it only stands to reason that, manifestly, by all objective standards, since by

Various accountabilities, we are not nearly so left alone, not to mention rejected, not to say spurned anymore, although albeit only quite recently, that perhaps we are entering into, as they say, a period of reassessment. "Tightly recap after each use." The Elector of Peekskill. Ability

to set and hew to priorities.

II.

Then, the big death. Someone's doing. Onto the lap of the Bureau. What does the ham say? Must be kidding if you think I'm going to give you my telephone number. A genius for going pale. See through by dissembling. The look of components which later took on so much of

The foreground therein, then, as only the most hypothetical place to set it all. I have precisely what you need. The half clogged street. "Be a man among men." The problem with sitting home waiting for the agent to call. False morning. Just drop the keys out of the window in a sock.

Fomentive post numerous conjunctive dicatalyptically derived. All the ships at sea. Panglossian optics. Dumb show. Crash course. Where the skin used to be. Red dogging. Bellying up. The sooty grid of the island. A silent E. Unconditional Surrender Frannie. Boulevard to the digs. The

Course of what seems now increasingly as a sort of desert of years, it had become almost routine, to feed, to square off against, to, as it were, steel oneself against, which, now, by the slight virtue of the decrease in ferocity. Alarm, office, luncheonette. Did you have a book or a

Magazine in mind? Racing leathers. Their wives sat back and rolled their eyes. The sole survivor. One went back to law school. One is laying back in the sticks teaching stovemaking. The only one still with a beard. Window envelopes. Unusually rich and aromatic. You *will* like it and come

Back for more. Adjusted gross receipts. Green light. Live freezer. Permanent non cling, 100% banlon, opening can be worn front back or side. Jumping cribs. How their whole day is geared, all 24, to that one hour onstage, all the motel smashing, Corniches in pools. Barney's not

So smart. On me. Erase fodder. Always so tired, at first I thought it was your diet, then, all those drugs, now you eat salads and smoke cigarettes, and still nod out. The semi-distinguishable shambles of trying to point out something that was never really not there. A dent where once

A lobe. Two make arbitrage. One turned out to be NY's top aspirin jingle coiner. Day of purchase to day of redemption. Three months in London in maryjane shoes. Quite an actor after all; certainly not on the strength of his good looks. Frisson of hair trigger Grenoble fain tail im-

Manent hoof maker lanky dalliant noumenon scandales remanding knock blea y gapping droves listing starred. Dashing Dan's unassailable. Now you want to give it all up for another. Raving quart. A petite cinerama. Unstringed dalliance. Another writes MASH episodes in Cen-

Tury City. Just how long do you think you can go on without me? The disused tunnel. Developmental limp wrists. A pension of virtue. If I just wanted to stay high I wouldn't have come downstairs. A glancing cuff. I'm waiting for the letter. The bashful poitrine. Not even if you paid

Me. The waiting, swaying over the barred way, quaking gulfs, a dirtied article of endearment, nonessential, into the twenties, without a stamp, I tried to forget, they did almost everything, a standard diversionary feint, this doesn't matter much anyway, the gem, the chiffon, the sloe,

The league of attaining dissolution. No reason not to tell you. Red Cross and USO installations. Hispano Suizas make me giddy. The quality of entropment. I can't be bothered to respond to those sorts of statements which, if you would be awake enough to realize, are the kinds of things

Which get thrown at us with such a monotonous depressing repetition, albeit not so frequently, or arrogantly, or 'from,' the same, or the same sorts of people that over the years have increasingly found themselves in what we wanted to think of as indefensible predicaments of their own.

Would like to shut him out of it also, if they could. This time I'm not ly-ing to you. Onset of kith. The Ecstasy of Theresa. Starting out near blows, buying for eachother. A Gale Storm impression. The dunnable mapped presentational demonative breaction discanting chinstraps

Disingenous mocked disdain masquerading in the trappings of clear sighted worldliness. Cordite sheets. If it were only, or nearly, a matter of how much time you were to be found in that position. Stasis majeure. I just wanted to make sure I'm not the one who catches it all. But whetted

To an expected sense of affirmation, a scouring assumption, a warping up of the interior correlatives, in the mundane guise still. A hemostatic entrance. Transferance smarts. Fungoes. Dingbats. Sudsheads. Stripes. Rubes. Tunnel folk. Elbows. Boneheads. Sure she'll be your friend. A

Skill you don't drop. Pat internalization. I engineered it for no other reason than to impress you, somehow. On the up and up. Slingback fadeout. Sarajevo zips away. Misbegotten congealation of debasements that has through no one but me, on the odd evening or weekend, the

Slightest utility, or need or sympathy for, as then, unfortunately I found myself with even more thrust upon me of those sorts of unavoidable, unforseeable, moments of *life* that even I, in all my possible pessimism,could have ever predicted or planned. By the by. If gently

Persuasion doesn't succeed. A lanky and amiable attendant. I had it right here a minute ago. Thanks for the kid. Cannibalized from an old Philco. Soon your breathing gets quicker and more shallow. The coin of that realm. The way you really have to sit down, get earnest, and spend

Some time giving strokes, to expect anything, any sort of special pitch or honing of the rarified indicators. Mr. Zildjian. Someone pressed it into my hand downstairs. You think you are so smart. Grizzled credit manager. Sleep or wake? If I had a dollar for every time some joker

Asked me that question. Corset training. It is yours for the asking. I wish just once I could get through to you, make you see, I really don't want to be someone who comes to mind every time your name comes up. Uzi's by the bushel. More like a love rhomboid. A neural possessary.

The funniest thing since the pigs ate their little brother. Maybe someone will invite us out for some lunch. You think I'm paying for any more of this? Soporific pistolero. If this doesn't convince you of the sincerity of my intentions, wait until you see him in the morning. Swarms crouched

Around Union Square. Like two untamed. He won't go for that. A word to the wise. A skill you don't soon forget, either. Working their forms furiously. I wanted to say that by the end of the year I had done more with all this or that time, that I had more to show for it, than this little

Misery. A case of paroled development. A cowlick that effaces itself. A suspension in trading. Soda jukes. Keep going around telling those stories. Spent ink. I forgot about those shirts. How little of the expression of desire truly *emerges* through the dust of a legacy which as a

Stable *soluted* combination whose residing senses lent themselves, by the lights of those who fancied they wanted to know, to the bank of the bearish presumptive, as an outcome of the approaching juncture, such as, or was, as an expectation that having arose between them, was still to

Be searched out, lying undisturbed, where it had been discarded. Some morning you might wake up, east of the Perdanales. Egg on the face. If you are shy, there are various aides to be jogged. Headed for trouble. It's only a flesh wound. Both sides of his mouth at once. When the diaries

Are published, then we can always go to court and, until then, they can shit in their pants. We used to call them Craterface and Tripod Legs. An infectious groan. Debbie abhors it. Please don't touch that one. Two gats. A vast, former street car roundhouse taken over by the telephone

Company; soiled abandoned wedges from the early sixties, musty links to the Berkshires; beds set up everywhere, merchandizing tags removed from the articles, trying not to look out of uniform. A toothy unbegrudging former correction officer. Dismal showing. The Stet im-

Printed on the forehead. "Let's start all over again, this will be year Zero. Everyone get out of town, now." Promises, the limp on the progress, I mean, I wanted to hear everything, not in any way to pass judgement, as if one could remain or could stand aside from things we saw.

We decided we needed to break through the walls and take over the neighbor's as well. The courage to throw it all away. An excuse a doorman might come up with. The kind of monumental or monolithic throw weight bandied about currently. Cantilevered rebuffs. One traffic

Light from here to Kansas City. The kind I knew from childhood. Remove to insert tap. The price of a simple goodbye. The immanatized eschaton. Shirt and pants. I don't want you to think I'm introducing an unwarranted element. That point in an illness when one has been sick

Long enough for the more pleasant ameliorating aspects of incapacitation to have worn off, long enough to find oneself more than a little bored with the routine of it, the worse of the symptoms, though not all of them, having abated, and the monotony of the condition, pre-

Recovery, in bringing a certain blindness to the underlying missing robustness, the essential 'lack' of health, often leading to, as it does here, to that state, that time, the scene when the restless invalid, having decided to summon up some residual or supposed restored, new found,

Reserves of strength, proceeds to roughly cast off the constricting blanket of the sickness, and proceeds to engage in some patently foolish, often excessively public, activity, going out and dancing and drinking, going out for a not so innocent brunch, so that just at the point where he was

About to turn the corner, with complete recovery only a matter of days away, the adventure precipitates, *naturally*, as a matter of course, a return to the condition, in fact less a re-succumbing to the old complaint than an opportunity for it to gain a second wind, or even, better, turn

Into something more virulent, and throw itself, its force, against the decimated susceptible, wreaking, often, more havoc than the original onslaught. Dreamy pursuit. More than ego. It wants to return to the jungle. Barely, like a Delaware corporation. As good a reason as any for

Punching him out. Plutocrat. Imbroglio'd. I had in mind something older, wider, filmier in black less pre-written less formal less tunnel like more attractive of attention. Here I am doing all of your old dishes. "I don't want my hands in any more commercials. No more good *pours.*"

The way a family name enters the dictionary. Bringing along a sledge. Tell them "nuts." Does begin counting with naught, 'which odd, which even?' They keep the leaves in the main compartment and the gourd in the ancillary, they're always chewing on something. I

Wondered if you really thought I was as evil as all that. The Coogan law. If I thought this was what I wanted, I would have gone fishing. Coterminal muff. Phlanges. The city line. Cowboy style, as the term is applied, as in, taking several bystanders along with the intended, *cowboy*

Style. Hunkered down. Eminently bored. Junkers. Lignite. Miniscus. Nobodaddies. Overboard. Primogeniture. Quondam. Riddled. Scapula. Quit claim. Timbre. Uranian. Vinegar Joe. Winsome. Xeroxy. Vapid. Walpurgian. Veloute. Younger. The yclept, an underlying anx-

Iety that to engage in any half way explicit revelation of the actual or verbalizable workings of the mind at writing would only serve to expose the paucity, the threadbare quality, an absolute absence of profundity. Latitudary. Accented apparatus. The eyes have it. A total lack of respect.

It could have been coincidence. Why is he sitting home, stalwart mole? The arches of a showgirl. A takeover artist. Closed end leases. Where the fortune really came from. A complete inability to 're-wind' and elongate that sort of contemplative industrialization that was drilled in-

To the thinking around the "stuff" that poems were made of. And, still wanting, finally, to keep up the role and the posture of that, to himself, and others, unsure, he turned to another sort of organization that, at first, in its fixation upon another fancy, what seemed formally as blank a

Superstructure, in roles shifted away the burden from the areas of selfhood he felt he was so unlucky so as to have *wasted his time* pursuing for so long. Eventually, of course, there was another self-unmasking, and he found himself with no other option, he thought, save somehow

Modelling himself after one of his contemporaries, or, even better, he found, several of them, in such a way, hopefully, so, on the one hand not to attract any notice, or at least overt comment, and on the other, perchance, somehow to ensure his place among the company, of this at

Least he was sure, in which he belonged. For, was he not at least as in possession of his faculties, as ready with a carefully turned phrase in the proper circumstance, as generally sensitive to the true pathos all around him, and neither blessed nor cursed with particularly more or less blind

Spots in his reasoning powers as any of his *friends*? It was just that, as he remonstrated with himself over and over again, he was sure that it was so much harder for him than any of the others to simply get the words out and on the page. He *felt* them inside, it was just impossible to get them

Out. He thought, he was sure he saw it in his work and feared others did as well. Beaming caliph. The kind of person, it turns out, who knows a little about a few things. At this point, the soiled hem of the memory. The eye at the top of the thirteenth step, looking toward the East, some

Scrubby vegetation at the base of the pyramid. No matter how carefully, one doesn't see the wall breathing. The impecunity of the strategy. The point was not how frightened we were, but how used we were getting to that state of affairs. The dosed settlement. I've thought I've seen you

Several times since then, improbable as it seems. A bit overboard. The sort of uncritical rage we once directed at closer targets. Paging extirpation. Like feet under the table, some gestures do not call attention to themselves. Had taken in. A real talent for grasping at straws. Bone of

Contention. I'd like a look in your files. New trends in blister packs. Courted, amassing. All I want is for you to get that thing out of my apartment. Never forgetting one's true mission on this earth. Accented on the little people. The way no one says street or road or avenue after

The street name or adds it to addresses on letters. There were precise shadows, fallen between the ribs where, in the time usually associated with the age, they were promptly forgotten. Anamorphic, descending over conversation, enshelling the feelings and glances in a discantation.

The later memoranda. Rowing to the party. A recourse, a featured soloist. The daggered cards. Height famine. I always go to New York to buy. An exhilarating domestication. The cast and crew. Making sure to include one dinner between every two lunches. More than a penchant.

The swimming pool. That you can please yourself sometimes. Well adjourned. "Tlingit Tom." Mortagee's turn. The amiable slab. An internal quotient. Sidestepping how-to. Model remotes. If you could walk a mile in his Lucheses. The page, the flats, the type, the expression on the

Mail face. Something like a Social Security number, in that you could have called me anytime. Rather quiescent regarding the original. Words that you would come across, in your world. If you announce it to enough of them, you'll be shamed into following through. Ritual assumption.

Everything I have learned, on a scale of one to ten. A teleology *where* betters. Shape growing, like a rent in the curtain of security. As it fills you up, wind in your conversation, gliding you up a curiously admixtured swell of certainty, that whatever you hear or may be called on to

Respond to, will, by some incomprehensible 'determination' that may in fact depart as swiftly as it appeared, but, during the tenure of its sway, afford an effortless avenue and inventory or accessibility, of registration—a swiftness posing as a calling up, a summoning, all,

However, tossed in with a sense that all the felicitous conjunctions and freshly raised up synapses, arching over both you and your, in a sense, audience, as well as the *improved* links between your first and outer layers of Presentation, the responding self, and the you that the former

Calls, as it were, upstairs to, leans on, makes liberal use of when possible, that all of the upgraded, newly harmonizing connections, are things progressing forward toward you, somehow a change in the pressure of the atmosphere you swim through, a *trend* that, for some

Reason, is picking you up and bearing you along in its train, not so much with any destination 'in mind,' as in some at the moment largely indeterminable 'direction,' for how long, and yielding what satisfaction or ultimate deficit, likewise, as of this time, remains largely unforeseen.

I didn't want to call them, I wanted them to call me, while I was still awake. Deigned not to recognize. Are you going home in a few years? Duoserve. A tame distance. The judgement of time springing not from any sum of application but out of the weight of all the 'staggering' in-

Volved. Finding the transfigured. Raked with those 88's. The same personality steeples and hurdles. Able to direct any flow of description towards standards and representations of bathos. What pass for fantasies, where we would be now if we'd kept going at that clip. Yammer-

Ing at the vault. As I shook it an ominous drop expelled itself down through a seam at one of the corners. "Literarily, it isn't how much you owe, it's how you string out the payments." Roanoke. Flax. Signed landscapes, unroomed, touring the codes, mundanity, the percentages one

Has to be willing to accept. Eventually you'll have to go out and lease one of your own. Racing home from each party and writing it all down. A commital. Mr. Moto Takes A Photo. The dollar standard. Quickstepping. As if it come straight from the smoke all around, sit down, blow

Off some steam. Who devastate their thumbs. Does one, any more anyone, stop in the depth of an evening, and look back, does this kind of reliving, a somehow 'waiting' mode of reduction, an 'aside-I' demonstration, ever find its way through the aging pulls and wraps we

Throw or allow to be drawn across the shoulders of our 'moral effort?' "Voice, unrelenting, over and through the wall of standing or propped upright humanity, the entire audience swayed, as one, 'done upon,' recipient wills, an acknowledgement to this Voice; and this room we had

Thrown ourselves into, dark, smokey, seeing no more than a body or two ahead, as one of our number leading us linked armed in a line aimed through the swaying throng, toward that Voice, worming our way to the 'stage,' the far end of the former strip club, I, I confess, found myself

Weary of the bodies I found myself pressed up against and broke my link in the chain and just tried to settle myself in place, keeping in unobtrusive touch with my billfold, with no particular desire to force myself to the front, best, it seemed, to let myself rock with the rest back

And forth there, washed by the Voice and the rest of the music; my eyes let themselves close, the 'refrain' swelled, I thought I was somewhere far away with someone else, a long time ago; time passed; then someone spilt something on my arm, my eyes opened, jolted back, and, thrown

By my sudden start, momentarily leaning against the swell of the rest of the audience's rocking and swaying, out of synch with the crowd, all unawares, I caught sight of her. A mere body length away, all in black, I could reach out and touch her, singing directly into my eyes." Colum-

Biana. Mr. Chase's classroom. Paddington. The notorious Five Points. The ability or apparent license, that is, the allowance for an appetite, to be able to return, letting by harboring, generally betokens a lack of pressure, something akin to market forces. Mechanically estruable

Signal. Misty shrubs, fluorescent blocking marks, lingering boom mike. A derailed evening, one breakdown at a time. The kind of posing you suggest. Grazing through the party. It gets soiled from just being looked at. Teaching Boney a lesson. Still and sparkling. This has got to be the

Sulieman expostulating. Like a pitcher with a lot of stuff left, which before I made it to the city, the house before the gates, a conversation in which all the talk is not enrosed, a petulant charm. What seems most regrettable is not the lack of savoir faire but their mystifying inability to

Recognize it as such, your subtle bulldog-like. Kind of traffic we usually don't see around here. Open house, a mask of *let's get on with it.* The basic fear that he would think she hadn't. Verbatim corporation. Ohio-Sealy. The common hydraulic. Lifting call capacity. In the proceedings

Entitled. Hibernia, foils. Closures. Acclamitizing. Travail. Pickup. Hesperidian. Scalloping. Half recumbant. Bootless. Mardi's. Scored. Nattering. Proctorial. Dolmen. Brang. Loping. Stychethemic. Jatted. Gaston. Auguecheek. Reticule. Variegated. Gobelin. Stamens. Cupola.

Fram. Gag. Hops. Condensor. Ribboned. Elemo- lago. Corroborative. Woof. Authoritative. Driller. Tuned. Posting raffine. Crake. Jasper. Testingly. Gleem. Ruminative. Binge. Fain. Lustral. Pons. Descant. Forked. Mind. Duod. Gusto. Carpathian. Nobe. Part-healed.

Redoubtedly. Captivation. Instrumentality. Lissome. Stallworth. Dispatched giantism. 'Flaired.' On-stance. Kalpa. Declassification. Paradism. Remittance. Flocking. Gainsaid. Man-number. Spode. Ex-culpatory. Minions. The Flat Head People. Rumble. Signatories.

Domicile. Gamely. Scarified. Rating-digest. Foment. Vlad. The Glines. Tolerably. Glassine. Rinky. Morgify. Soft-ship. Adorn. Basted. Melanomaniac. Laff. Garnets. Just-side. Clasp. Blacked. Smatter. Gloriful. Raft. Sloane. Particate. Rookies. Mealy. Nabob. Bled. Renter.

"Dwezel." Alum. Walleyed. Nubbing. Trucked. Sharped. Cuff. Scouted. Anack. Foresook. Goaled. Corruptive. Veil. Clefts. Flume. Calistoga. Ordure. Stonily. Ward. Slatting. Unchastened. The epitomal breakfaster. Abreacting. Consumption. Tea y. Ushers. Optioned.

Fraternization. Perm. Haspels. Bowdlerized. Rosters. Knackery. Stax. Abash. Mantis. Symp. Horology. Pranks. "*Unhappily*." Mortise. Chasen. Regle. Bibled. Inhaler. Opcrose. Heeling. "Dukish." Tarred. Not subway rumble down there. Anchorite. Wreathing. Paced. Ag-

Gregative. Twill. Mans. Kicked. Fingering. Reprobate. Which is your voice? Mattered. Starker. All of me. Flying squad. *The Inter-Wool Secretariat*. Confessions are just more trowel work. Roiling. I don't need to wait for an answer. Alexandria's soup of expressways. I forgot where I.

Something you wouldn't do even with your best friend. Warring branches. Practical recourse. I always wanted one. Easy tuning. What do you hide, besides your drafts, that you aren't ashamed of? On the zero or the one? Get me the founder. Red neap.

Careless Eyes

No excuse
at table
roseate, spin dry
appeal shellac
the Narrator's cruelty
to get your bearings
"sanhedrin"
case hardened
capability, green
emolument
wisteria choked
overpass
the only thing which
        is never named
unspooning
"vanishing cream"
oral surgery
english finish
afounder
caret
learned unease
anthrax
        coupon
taped on paragraphs
unacknowledged
        stray
finisterre
hi gloss
stet
a closer semblance of waving
with the eyebrows
I feel my heart
else
astair

Inwood
confound
totalling
          spanned
the exercise manual
seeing it on all of them
          means there must be a law in effect
why did it take me this long
shock bonnets
slap happy
legitimist
greaves
hair relaxer
ex offender
celebratory error
ajax
eccentric orbits
hazel tone
modern annunciators
hitless
the mordant climate
less the clarified
tool box
bootless
fly tie
wishing we didn't have
I tried, I called
unfailingly
staked out
scale remover
gap in the curtain
message volume
toothless rushes
adage

trapped onstage
nu vinyl
wardrobe
when everything starts to seem as
        heightened as
afraid to sleep (?)
turf builder
narrative frustration
the saxophone
blotter
man hours
panoply equipped
is paved with
full time equivalent
durst
where are you
loop the, warrantless
don't leave your labs
college ruled
what's fort worth
hoving over the place
apartment relay
the name's
addressing the bars
common bible
key grips
delancey
careless eyes
sweeps as metaphors
takes my breath
your basic combo
routine parse
inky boiling
from sumatra come worrisome

croyable yellows
manumission
purchase on
silenium announces the
just lucky
pound
collateral perles
I came by to see
understand anything (?)
mountain gears
who would have thought it would
carminative pity
who do you have to
self rising
dreadnought
someone running on an interstate
the division tables
weeded
hop to it
"picking iron out of your liver"
"coastal artillery"
what you think you know
what you don't think about you think
    you know so well
roaring spring, pennsylvania
Keats talks about America
the middle harps
may cause some discoloration
too much chasserei
biologically collusive
the dock of elapsed
penny tomes
lost gags
the house by the steps

nothing doing
dutch interruptions
unreserved downing
how quickly they
carrying a patch of yellow
keep several rolls on hand
lips as a loop
the modern companion
just when I was ready
while I had been
        down where I was then
the container of the argument
drawn from
felloed
of a degree it seemed
bel airs
I think the sense
berlinetta
getting to know better and better
out of the selves
high streets
between what we could
        possibly bring up
johnson era
the bulk of seconds
I would have if I
levelizers
when were you
accreditation
bring if there
halogen
likely to be glad that
under normal expectations
boat tail

as if reminded by prevailing
burl
to place under
to discover (to wit) next
close
doored
implying w/o
to chance on the street
calculating without
harupsicate
or circuitry
remind with elements
expected retinue
nothing too circumstantial
developing the parallelism
to entertain
ideating surfeit
try
agentry
trappings
against the
referred as bathos
in the car of
motifs
      generative and wishful
somnolent barracks
owning up
informing for
firing the remains
withholding as
level produce
H O scale
as a blob
eels

raining
slo mo
farm house
about the same
SAE
east lansing
federalist style
river front
plumber's helper
shape of an
        awesome boxcar
calling out
with a tendency
        for boiling over
or trying on the
don't hold it against me
suitable for blackmail
an ice cream parlor anyone
        could be found in
a name (like)
cousintry
"appointment and disappointment"
the way everything coheres, warnings,
        the grit that flew in the window
        and struck your forehead
presentation sets
scissor kick
beneficial finance
I thought I might call
better to
concurrent sentences
treating as face
carved in from
diplomacy where one hand

for either ear
dough boys leap up
what difference does it make
    now that we are talking
the planar virtues
a drum orchestra
to press is akin to
causal chic
gendarmerie
eighth floor
mone han statuary dormez freighted
    rote stedg cone section orn am
    empi acle tat cabinetry deck
    appeal merrying tendon broom
    readability finger heddle food
    shearer any rapacious hone abarth
timetable for impending
fils de roi
handsignals or
airless sprayers
palatable contraction
eyedropper
pontine
collapsible
local drumming
for the lack
    of a trailer hitch
tape delay
"horn out"
fierce trowelwork
on yr head
isn't Hornsby
    school age (?)
pooled

message units
scientistic wrench
middie
all that netting
finally someone called the
decals
hoard toppler
yellows from
how it'll all
           add up later
trying the jalousies
excited surfaces per se
m a b s t o a
cutting corners
which is commonly adjudged
           as fronting for
really want to do
stooped partaking as rabidly
maybe not as East as
when you open in the morning
the muffler king
terms that even a
not that it was not yours to
auditron
brainy
salad
montecruz
the detach
coal shouldn't irk
besides Muscovites
besmirched
pocket memo
committees of correspondence
mechante

the end of the line up
not that button
pied
scoping the park
decommission
nonbenevolent
poste restante
canvas courts
tier
d k w's
facilitators
downtown for a switch
infected rags
that everyone's thinking about this
    all the time, which they are
maddox
pole (position)
the sound of someone pounding on
    a door early in the morning
I used to think that I was
    trying to recall
why not treat yourself
bluff
checkered
just to see what prehensile effects
lunching
irritated
figure eights
hearing the soap dish
to make ends meet
port of call
appendices
(stuffee likes to ride
    below the waterline)

by the rate of
"I don't care what they say"
returned, cast down, the cinder floor,
        the hope forgotten, the arrival of
        the machine, the image of what is
        refused, disallowed by its semblance
        (the ruse of the twins, the disrupted
        feast)
recusal
roughage
me and my shadow
horse and carriage
the thicket of bare short trees, the ruts
        in the muck, hissing from somewhere
who moved among them
organized in a matter of months
find under every
the same, just like each
due
trap rock
I liked your phone number
this is called a face off
fitful rest on a cot
right as if next door
a falling object
part of us which apparently
finding myself inadvertently
lower incidence
when an overflowing sink clued
the increasingly rare ability
to take the fall
uncovering consumption
world owing us at least a spatter.

Disclaimers breed
the unextinguishable nub
developing "events"
as Swiss as
usually tarrying
malefactory, genius
grains
the harsh of great
as I began to comprehend
        the extent of your grip
dynastic balloons
relieving the cities
the elevated light
taxed
if this was a "judicial" detour
which wouldn't have thought
        would have been noticed
like that   a time   that's like
        later   the rutting   litter
        of the   bored swim   as moody
        tries   spare   bravery in the
cinching up all along the
augur
more to your liking
wilsonian
specificatory
it isn't
dyes
one of your handkerchiefs
a big deal in those parts
shake down cruise
smiling boyars
this is what I say to
        your shooting brake

country assizes
diagnosis careerism
stripping in gratification
as if brown shoes
you were right
a suit
in awhile it came to me
prey to the common
as likely now as
        how many years ago
sort of climate we are used to
on the up and up
self starters
give them the high sign
who was turned as
        easy as the yellow pages
keen
whose keeping track
every day forgetting as much
a bouquet of
in on it
warning track
wire admirer
the outlying material, areas
        of a world being scuttled
excuse me
        yours for the weekend
cities service
mouth of the hudson
precise ground strokes
gatling
the veiled benefactor
caught in the depths
could not help exclaiming

on the pad
"her eyes"
cotton bond
secret factory
that side
"I went over to the brigadier"
biting off more than one can chew
a cough away
anti jamming
in the violet
inertial guidance
castles in Yonkers
circulatory bane
dutiful
green plan
the Canaletto's shadow
        on the wallpaper
toll clerk's disbelief
undersea service
delivery of the office
Mesmer's watch
short take off
dottier by the hour
living again in
        the recitation
reinforced
apothygm
domestic measures
appurtenance of so called
the building   compatible gauge
        court bloods   lesion in
        the totals   paper money
        these hairs mean   w/pig
        eyes on liberty st.   res-

olutely disheveled   street-
babies
the world city
trading in their traditional
I recognize it, these are words
training and arms
the great games
penchant for what
could be called banditry
errant
answerable
a grammatical sock hop
thinking perhaps without
any justification
the air quality
anti tanks
the toys on the rug
wind breaks
in case
woebegone redstone
call it foolishness
once the provendor ground
in the mill of
a policy of encouraging
the real reason why
the mail takes so long
don't make a fuss
actually lowering the temperature
these are the only pants
to rename an isotope
denying the place
storm sewers
actually putting down some cash
the aegis of any sort of order

really getting some for ourselves
the lubricant
recognition routine
your bridge
incomplete ownership
the pages like to be
the interest of
        certain highly placed
stopping for
the way we all resemble
mental supply
blinded by the petrol
compensatory shrinkages
didn't recognize their exquisite
        manners for what they really were
on the lap of the
wide shadow at the edge of the park
looking with eyes that are not ours
necessity appurtenance
ready to grow two more
the failing conciliatory
through the old part of the city
impaired facilities
drophead
this is your all-season
it as a minus
can use half a pair
the telegram of our
Marsha
beefed up
mud baths for
villa
assistance from which
        unexpected corner

complements
white sam browne
our old h.s. cell reunited
madcap
with timely
because you own one you think
the house of
1000 shirts
aliases for this
the inscription on the lintel
adamant
losing things
two faced ciphers
all used to live in
tents, like these
courant
on her, below the
forgoing the evening
the scent in the
you can always
tell from the logo
less clannish
a golpe
that all this
excitement could
pretend it is a swimsuit
connected in some way
remaining from
the days in the trees
the friendly paint
curve of the gasworks
order of attachment
a clean breast
who introduced the practice

the way the act
        itself is called up
where before some casual
        sort of identification
either it gets blocked out
a fundamental consanguinity
        among the descendents
the short fall of the fulcrum
a little birdie who sits in
        the assistant commissioner's
it was the vertical, but
        to suggest anything further
on the arm of
planning haze
clerkly luxury
on the bridge as she
de-de
fastness
think of the signmaker's equity
swap by the brewery
here and there
the pop of the saws
here, she said, drawing aside
and sporadic
"this is my"
to see again
discernable lack
relief from
capstan
roof top parties over
        contested jungle
the rounderel
source possibilities
ability for hatching

a certain sort
sanction
vision in earth tones
resisted
apprehend
often results in the
the colony
singlehandedly
an element out of this world
one's own utensils
so many hours before tiring
preference in these climes
heavy water
the feckless
the sense that makes
        you want to
a chase in the street
strop
a tour of the plant
rheumy
on the southern outskirts where
        storage tanks once dominated
an arcade where white jacketed
the settling rubble
wind sprints w/strom thurmond
the company once grossed
the sort of aerial formations
an obvious tectonic
with the topographic prostration
appreciation of the
rebabbiting
whoever thought about it
toastmaster
or feels necessary

pillarful
sedanette
no recourse but to return
no free tickets
phaetons
negotiable
factory verse
sidemounts
gorgeous Nevada
policy
        relic
club sandwiches
dunnable
for any temporal extent
loaded
wood pressure
deauville in redi-mold
government fleet
ring tripped
fog king
garnish trimmed
skirts
glove boxes
sources of disjunction
johnson
signing the writ
an issue of
overland
        speedsters
subject to the
windsor
belvedere
greene
saloon

so the question could easily follow
tourer
lalique fixtures
in touch with
Floyd Clymer's Skoda
fract
empress style
cibie
prop wash
on the trunk
don't you sometimes say to yourself
            someone was probably listening in
as the combinatory
eyeing
running feet
whose money
five basements
not the same really
could decay down to
flexible plaits
always carry enough
            to at least bail yrself
a fitted
all entreaties
greying with velocity
factory maintained
cloth magnet
undercoating
I see you looking back
detune
who hailed a cab like
for the time being
captain of the watch
deliberate gaffes

needless to
divvied by the months
dublin askance
the terms you signed
enjoins
this rare abbreviation
machine sibling
worldly humidity
membership card to
        the human race
kramden
enough time
juvenate
carbine williams
overdrawn
seen this before (?)
grape line
like a lot of actors
thank the wax
flying spurs
like a tailor
plimsoll mark
rose lashing
in the ribbon windows
coston light
bombination
mohs scale
gymel
martyrish
lavage
the foot of tragedy
dabbling in occidentalism
rail and lake
mixed grill

think much (?)
steam, untidily
flight pen
time being
alliteratively clad
urbanauts
ask the milkman
surfacing gear
armenian survivors
zoot
to honey your words
the course of events
leave of
by a professional who enjoyed his work
drawn
shack
binomial
presneak
housings
templet
depended
notorious
in shop
filiate
redub
walking through her lines
cotter.

Like a plucked
not more than three
a machine for
whose hymn the condemned all

wanted pressing
test kit
commentless
activity within our
stone age
strong armed
outstayed
which tides
price-y
live with this
cleaning department
sphagnum
genuine replacement
kind to hands
guest experts
so that no one would guess
a prince of
your complaining
a crosshairs
more than important
throw weight
so arguable
sniffer
totally out of
sticky
private counties
the fifth
your grace
a friend of the court
such
the lot of
an instrumentality of the
the clock in the door
piney

sober
raft implement
that special
your sense
in bound
radiators
all in a hat
checking
(good) valise
a pile of
whose memory haunts me
tix
a method of training
manse up there
if only
sleeping compartments
drome
kind enough to take
ward of
dote
your ville
thankful for small
horthy
got enough
those words which are not yours
the part that picks up
wouldn't dream of
money honey
executive lieder
road racing
way time
addler
as new
as they wind onto eachother

if you really tried
oned
half repeated
whose ticket is punched
spurning dilutions
way station
hemmed air
out of laziness
torn out fireplaces
the way of all her
yr yodel
beaucatcher
slightly disagreeable
twelveness
sectoring
allie
fill er up
call by whatever
unpredictably dolorous
the pacemaker
whisper "causeway"
game all the
the signals
the line of clay
clothed off
try not to get
not to say all of
        these aren't yours
fructose
looking over
makes friends wherever
in the holler
running out of
your super

keyholders
the people's choice
camouflaged provinces in paraguay
the second time
tulle
words are cheaper
inspite of the
for the lodgers
to the senses
        most felicitous
midnight tidings
a change in air perhaps
invited to turn blue
mends fence
an object, like
        a delivery van
the planet itself
how could you forget
bad half
for the crowd
time sharing
self lighting
this club
concert of lockers
syndie
not getting to any letters
under the offshore
the house of
the resounding
the terrific sand
point of no return
the track record
dressed like a
area authoritites

I was wondering when you
        would make an appearance
the enclave on the
in restraint of trade
taking on the
less sated
raising irresponsibility
        to socially hitherto
bow man
eyeletting
this scheme of yours
drubbing
mealy fright
out of teeth
mimical turn
lone farm
discreet collector
your share in this mess
in the interests of your
high toppers
what do you pay for this much
tug of the compressors
standing by unable to believe,
        happening in broad daylight
swelling "chandeliers"
dropped like a wet match
the excuse for
begin to allow, then
the daily tribe
chaplain school
putting in a call
venous arrest
talk to the animals
merely contrite

making friends with your extremities
muscling out
glamorene
the foil of
aeacy
"frisian"
their gaunt attire
trust officers
shall a congerie
a cut in the hill
wind on the letters
paper flout
core, squared
on the strength of your
baalbek
souvenir images
incognizant
painting by the
a figure of a mechanic
someone's park
on the dot
wake of the prowler
responsive to misery
unregenerate,
      wharfside
obfuscation of contrast
bargain hunters
substitute enamels
what was left on the
      balustrade in the morning
can you (?)
resulting in the Solomons
calming up
fastest moving

garrulous charts
brown bales
a thousand from now
no basis in fact
kicked around
avoid shipping
how long can the stomach
a look inside her apartment
flying fish
sponsored by
the first foreign teams
"white barges"
grandfather embraced
        the schoolchildren
satisfying local demand
tempted to believe
slim in the South
new harrows
don't cooperate
hand picked
leafy apotheosis
suspect patience
ideals from abroad
to obtain confessions
some babies
your turn at the wheel
been up to (?)
conflict over a violin
life of the marrow
marks in the arms of the chair
what we are wanted
        to be impressed with
you call them, then
press not

vert, idle
string band
fencing
modiste
spare linen
great ten
have you now
service entrance
honor system
for andirons
gummed up
this globe of sorrow
way everyone
"raw" information
on rooftops
the dell
since they refuse
        to take the sign down
extraneous lucidity
no mange on this one
your tendency to instill
what it feels like
        to see it on the earth
approving lakes
something in her throat
the dejected street
fitting neatly into the routine
trailhead
a word from across
date bogey
front wheel drive
come over and look around
tipped in
suited for mass

notorious in the pursuit
is there another (?)
the following countries
has informed
too zoftig
fostered under the
hold for instruction.

Just
shad
lict
dace
banting
"nissim"
yr mines
chime
basal readers
gone-y
hard questions
mett
carbon head
lolled
knocker
sked
pas ici
"shoulder fountain"
map-ful
news cleanser
insurance pool
must roam
how this hair got here
lower west side

sled
palpable
    plates
driveaway
sponges
halft
krebbs
in the kip
working at tension
sweatshirt
carry
torme
"industrial slums"
facial tissue
yr window
by the door
flamina
on the
of accord
2 talents
w /a mirror
d o h c
charmed
jobs in jersey
stomach this
assistance
cain
maim
which
the missus
step
saddled
pitch
yr mixture

through walls
handle with
bunkhouse
mill
eyeballed
swain
tripped the
from hunger
twin grievances
blue hall
boring
chancellery
two times
introduction to knots
embue
an "unique" immensity
yr restive plaint
remembered loge
in the lane
with the skin
bender
chaw
green river
restrict streak
golo
unsharpened
drew
glimt
deplane
floater
bas
defeature
swell
prod

scowling
elmarit
the steps of the
jeep roof
closter
titling
bumping
crokers
irregular sevenths
famously enough
unsold
another society
convertible
at yr
subdued
bee line
undeposited
that tailing
yr bow
tighting
watered silk
midge
westy
medal
no boating
cosseted
your size
face value
naively
elbow grease
unreconstructed
haltingly, breadth
tack the interlocuters took
untempered

fellow traveler
between deaths
crept
flam
erringly believed he'd stumbled on
pownal
insulating pretext
in the same, the new
pared
sinuous package
the sweat of cash
inflection, bootless
appreciate thefts training
        stock melodrama swingtime
pleasance
unsure culprit
extra short
want to go
        out too
good way off
fenestrate
remote control
mercantile, solicits
finishers
stellar backdrops
only
        so much
die sets
interest from, not always similar
coached sizing,
        wise guys
blow in human farms
chip in
tell tale croup

sensibly
unique, bannister type
jitters
the needs behind the
detour book
president who (?)
I wished your playback
M.E.'s fawn Checker
had proved
the dosey do
sleeping porches
sweet and low
scores of thousands
potters
        parade
fine points
avoidance, cheek
of indemnification
about the bush
refrigerant which leaks
terrible to
business for these many
at a time when who else
like a haspel
terriers
munitions work
could, never
sense of a short lived republic
a lack of aberration and neighboring
biding their
laminar
productive
some headknocking
its reversed mountain seasons

where does this train
the opportunity
when the lines go down,
        or the settlers
in brief, the lack of time
no dismal
important notes
having to cross out
after the darkness
bottle tuner
page dimensions
or a maniac
what may be right
in the Adirondacks
your convictions
some little girl's favorite voice
wondering why you felt impelled to disclose
tonight'll
a ghost of
out of form
a chance
kind of
        not there
you—what knows
mess with
ordained repetition
price for
facing up to
before your were born
the problem with medicine
and the june bug
port training
which, if you
        cannot hold onto

trust alibi
production values
returning from the supposed fiction
the pale of settlement
duoed
rocky from the
the previous
satchel charges
if not as your
    own, at least
the effects of applied and
    continual doses of whatever emotion
radio serics
"rugged prairie looks"
familar cuffs
from an affectionate
    child playing with a
another decade's aerodynamics
might just be selling the rights
    along with the name and the
s'would
the years of your life
a voice not
to fool yourself in writing
a sort of benefactor
your department
for instance
once, when the nephew of the old man
because you should have told me
and when the deadline
found
the ability to choose the terms of
    the argument, like a letterhead
wishing a texas-sized

on your hands
by the
      entrance
sold the store
found cold
comply
why return at all (?)
the along of
stone age
I see
two sided is cheaper
must be included as a matter of precedent
featuring
had they the time for
the ability to sit for more than
I wish I had your
obdurate
most complete consumer complex
what do you say
      to the person who has
the corner of your eye
squatters
not the tribute of the
check out these
the short side of
sometimes there seems no sound choice
bought his voice for
      the exclusive benefit of
disclosing of executive agendas
for the want of some
extent of
disbursement of the patroon's effects
demise of high heeled
as easily as his new tailor

which were to realize upon maturity
unbelievable three week parties
subsidized canals
still heeding your
what's doing downtown
elastic mileage
the sultry adieu
after all
each and every
middle road to rejecting
the blue in the matches
chaired by the substitute
water damage
a superfluity
diction reruns
high romance, underwater interests
the public trough
no more rectifiable than the
          deed which in his youth
the derogation of
          any given dimension
none of that stuff, sonny
who use the brain
          during its down
deserves a ride out by the
blown up a bit
shortstops note
broken, I thinks it might be my
mal chance
the action of the filter
sleeping compartment revised
the betterment of your
where a magnetic compass
lazy

but neat
picked apart
lessee
accomplishment management
carbon sets
w/o siphon
worry about filling,
      first we set the margins
mud in flight
the hope of a
thrombosed
excepting real
not too party-ful in this
connubially addressing
receding cartoons,
      the spread of the cranes
the latest prize
application of "continual"
learns in a day or two
clears out sooner than
a name like that
not so far
from here
more as 'Becca'
how it is possible to tell
      more than a directional source
skipping the
necessitous returns which
headlights
the aces in the gruel
the index of contagion
traffic in souls
semi-adult
a constant library

getting
for your mobile
all in sweaters
would like to exchange the frame
assorted drones
a lot like
too evenly matched
to look
stained pedals
someone saying, getting used
            to almost anything, your get
feeling the weight of the map
historic pressure
leaving town
            or something
yr own
            nails
the desert corps
getting sick
by the waters of
in tow
wednesday afternoons
altar boys
not coordinated sufficiently
            to preclude the possiblity
the arrangement of the creeks
            under the modern cross streets
the amenities of disabling
resisting diagonal temptation
natural disaster
special high speed printout
one, any, half an argument
lack of appetite
            for instance

prey on the likes of you
densen up there
better thank
a natural 'response' to all that
for a song
open casting hours
an emporium of
what comes first
a plugged nickel
deaccessionist stance
an encre-y mold
the finite attribute
air disaster
a logical conclusion
infrequent visit to the boiler
in December
      when everything runs out
pain of well being
heartbreak of intuition
best you
the waste of the day
eduardo remembers the convertible
hissing soliloquy
try-outs
houndedly
june-ist
bad case of the
a linen notebook
donut shaped
generalized desuetude
desperately funny
cooling tanks
japanned trellis
brush hog

the cottage by the
trache
simpled
entr'acte
light on the
discovery motions
colony stalwart
whoso applies
apparent venues
gaunt   stantial
blush money
augured, boats
clear legging
fooled breakfront
bated cleanup
message headwaters
dyspeptic catch
nagging trances
arctic bungle
marred reservoir
shifting unelicited
unfair approach
save yr stubs
knot motive
weak galore
drought sock
radio leaguer
where for
page's hand
railroad etymology
tune y spector
half again
'waiting' allowance
un easy

caseable layout
fusion ticket
popular standby
aimless vendor
special tribute
cold plate
a supposed pastime
the thought of you
        heartless commuter
bolted rash
george's comparison
gamey mawking
paint in here (?)
hungry aptitudes
star crossed lessons
doted yield
plenty of notice
wordy sendoffs
whatever confidence
voice displeasure
platinum, I hope
one more than wide
clearing shacks
astonishingly uncontrolled
flank quoting
the shade of the craft
destined token
emptied hum
too much dough
wastrel cowers
kited vacation
bulgar loves
a subtile distance
rendering tractors

sponsor rule
sunning pointedly
meaning ration
class recognition
in (side) there also
movie stars too
indented bodied
crossing out
someone's farm
skeleton crew
dispense barely
flew the coop
tine, asking
selfconscious drift
all talk
scotched chore
not so fast
minding the store
unflappable visitors
whose streets (?)
welling bar
back burner
glad rain
hope caking
not a lack of choice
convoy charms
hapstances contend
scaling lights
original miasma
base tie in
exertion paved
version rut
dozens in lieu of
alignment doubt

moment to spare
the unentranced arrival
red letter
stormy years in
the sway of the North
    away from the sun
deriding concealment
half moons
able antenna
wanton flair
so much
dusty mail
once about
at the bottom of all
where you see the
    moraine in the wood
catch-all phylum
the long and the short of
where the fragment had embedded
years by the roadside
sizing it
economical decomposition
demeaning capital
screw loose
an ear for
a leak in the gene
the representation of verse
worn on the nose
commercial pity
without bothering to ask
would you
likening to
prediction cloak
unpointed

roundhead gifts
when one starts noticing
        in the corner of the eye
part and parcel
the respondent cloud
as the inactive mimics the
for a slight remuneration
insufficient call
in the clover
the snap of the banners
using who (?)
all the difference in the world
a language for your own
liking wrong parts
off and on at will
patented combination
signature
divided into lots
equivalent of a rangefinder
unnoted departure
prosodic miscegenation
get you used to
for the whole house
remaindered punchlines
lost in the stands
old get up and go
house afire
the thought of another morning
an unusual complaint
at home with the
a quick bite
rotary fire
breaking the phalanx
a fabric of lies

schofield barracks in the
says makes little sense
lack of choice in the matter
arrayed syntax
simply for the purpose of evading
something due
nothing down and
unbearably sensitive
misplaced dispassion
the trouble with depending on your
inapposite temperments
the emptying of the sea
malicious redundancies
respecting the niceties
no need to reseed
wanting to step on
the song of the diggers
finance by the sea
the last house on the left
romance of
the length of his tether
wreaking messes
hardworking clouds
price of a flight
what can he do for you (?)
a souvenir of the peninsula
jaunts to the cemetery
shipbroken
point of sale
rapid discoloration
wrapt in the misery
so much as a fare thee well
demoted lists
timing chains

great make believe
a true tissue
no dealers within
as good as a hit
false shards
debt service
poured w/o the aid of
a continuous slide
last days of this market
whatever you can get
an unwanted reprieve
waning to their accustomed
washed memorabilia
half again as many
where she used to prepare
to the blandishments
like no one's business
inducing breathing
secret additives
hoped for smoke
the brace of the current
those ditches
sun porch
in a dither
until losing the timbre
too much relaxation
a false ceiling
antigen captain
the lack of a job
tenor of response
no accounting for taste
a sure fire cure
the first palace
even mention

breezy deceit
removed from the registry
a serum for
anything you might have
here before (?)
great quotes
the fervor of a man half his
ends up pointing at you
part time restitution
the dawn of creation
amateur detectives
grates on my nerves
the resemblance is only
on good authority
a burn on the side
adjusted for high altitude
the only other dot on the
swells in the crowd
for your own purposes
harassing hitherto
no hands
ankled
hold on all of them
lensed
kick stand
a bay in the wind
never an early riser
you used to stay
stringing along
        multi-effrontery
dropping the domino
someone's precious collection
the fate of the wheel
littoral

incline, "nu"
"to the vault of paved heaven"
custom (ized)
parkway police
current events
liquid paper
down the world, in the
blare
draw bridge tenders
as one gauges
barely here at all
happy motes of dusk
a disconnected
as you were
canted lot
past the brushing.